I'm Reading About

I0888800

NORTH CAROLINA

The Tar Heel State!

GALLOPADE

by Carole Marsh

Printed and Manufactured in Peachtree City, GA., USA
www.gallopade.com

Book design: John Hanson

Editorial manager: Janice Baker

North Carolina is a great state.

It is one of a kind.

What makes North Carolina special?

Let's read about it and see!

NATIVE AMERICANS

Who lived in North Carolina first?

Native Americans did!

They moved around to find food.
They hunted in North Carolina's woods.
They fished in North Carolina's rivers.
They gathered fruits and seeds and nuts.

EXPLORERS

The first explorers came to North Carolina in 1524.
They came from the country of France.

Giovanni da Verrazzano was their leader.
He and his men were looking for gold and silver.
They also wanted a faster way to sail to Asia!

SETTLEMENT

A man named John White
came from England to America.
He started the first settlement in North Carolina.
He settled on Roanoke Island.

North Carolina was one of
the original 13 colonies.

Roanoke Island

STATEHOOD

North Carolina was the 12th state to join the United States of America!

Isn't it great,
to be a state!
I bet North Carolina
could hardly wait!

North Carolina became a state in 1789.

North Carolina
The 12th State
Here we are!

FLAG

I am the state flag.
I was adopted in 1885.

What colors am I?
Red. White. Blue. Gold.

Look at me.
What else do you see?

I fly high over the state of North Carolina!

MAY 20th 1775
N C
APRIL 12th 1776

CAPITAL

Say hello to Raleigh,
the capital city of North Carolina!

There is an important building in Raleigh.
It is the State Capitol.
North Carolina's laws are made there!

Capitol
Raleigh
Capital

SEAL

I am a seal,
but I am not the State Seal.
If I were, I would be very important.
I would be stamped on many official papers.
(Ouch, that might hurt!)

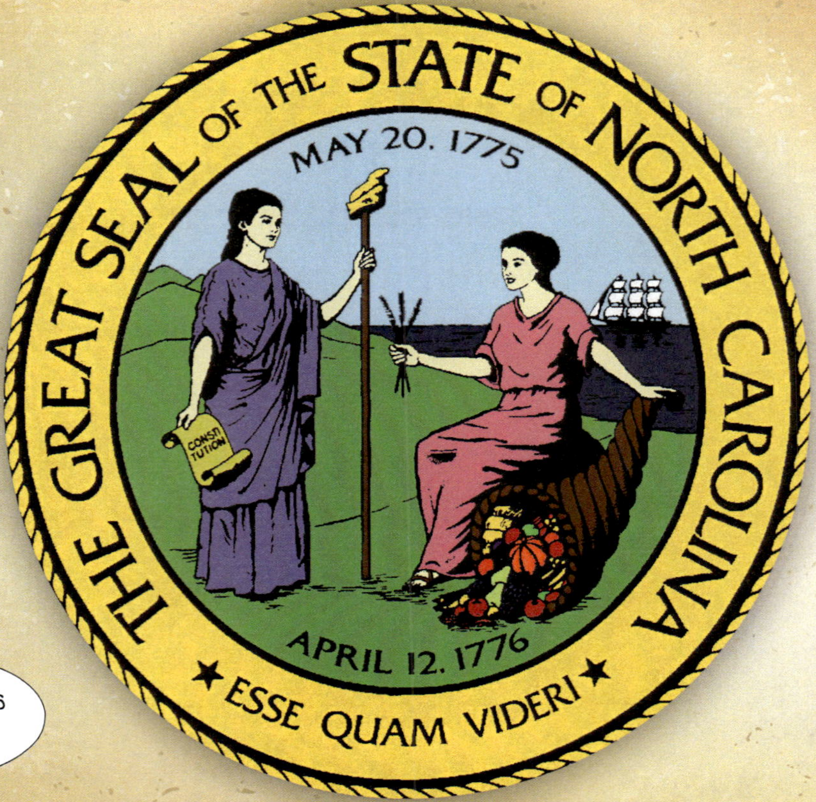
THE GREAT SEAL OF THE STATE OF NORTH CAROLINA
MAY 20. 1775
CONSTI TUTION
APRIL 12. 1776
ESSE QUAM VIDERI

Now, that's official!

NICKNAME

State nicknames are fun!
State nicknames are great!
They share fun facts
about each state!

North Carolina has several nicknames
One nickname is "The Tar Heel State."

North Carolina makes tar from pine trees
in its forests.

The Tar Heel State

1861-1865

THE TAR HEELS ROLL OF HONOR

NORTH CAROLINA, With a male population (military age) of 115,000 furnished 127,000 CONFEDERATE SOLDIERS

Lost 40,375 of her brave sons, DOUBLE the loss of any other state with 5,000 to spare.

FIRST AT BETHEL

FOREMOST AT GETTYSBURG

FURTHEST AT CHICKAMAUGA

THE LAST AT APPOMATTOX

"God Bless North Carolina"

R E Lee

BORDERS

Look at North Carolina.
North Carolina is in a region called "the Southeast."

North Carolina borders four other states.
Find them on the map!

Borders

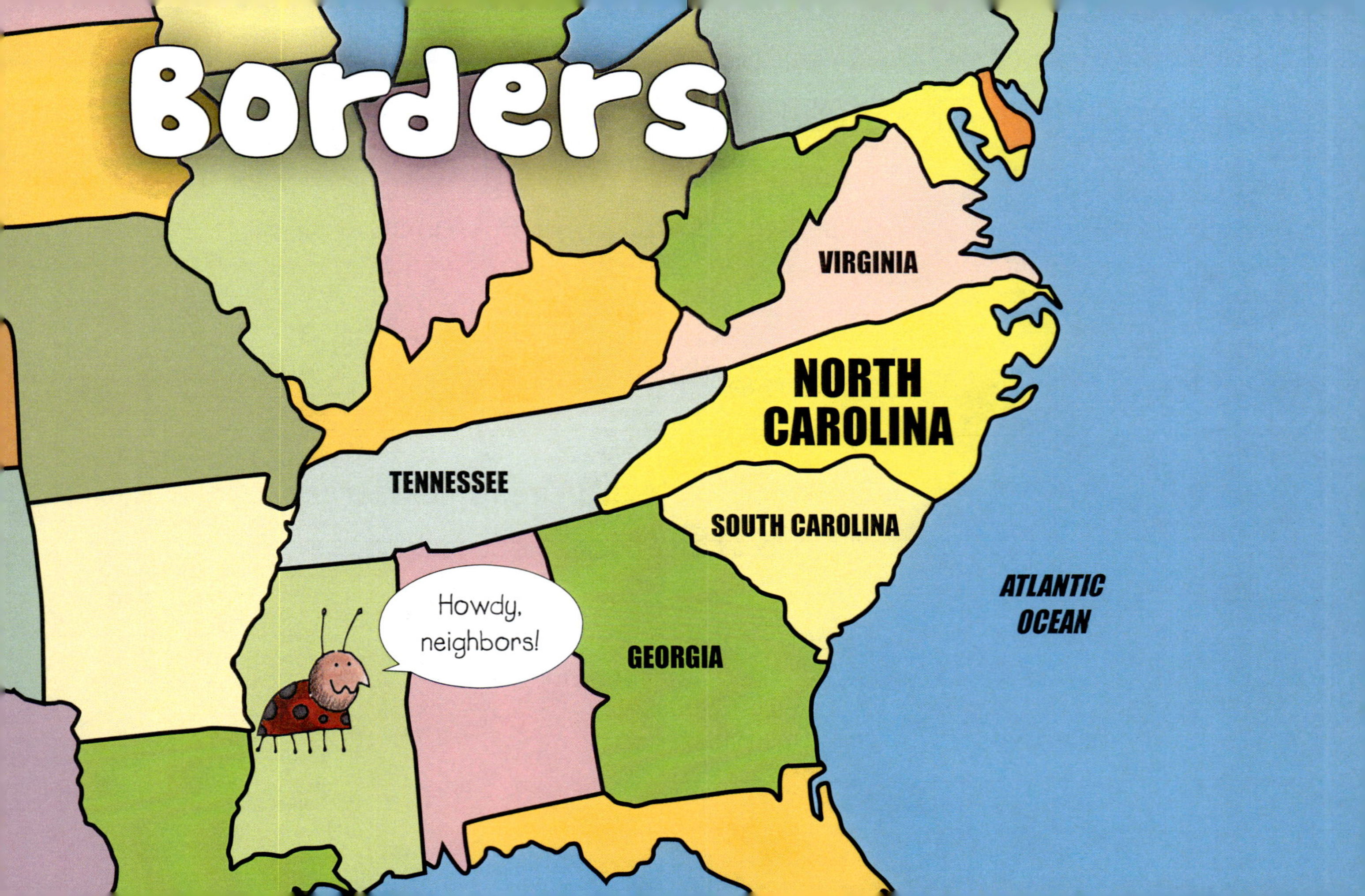
VIRGINIA
NORTH CAROLINA
TENNESSEE
SOUTH CAROLINA
GEORGIA
ATLANTIC OCEAN
Howdy, neighbors!

PRESIDENT

The President is the leader of our country.
He lives in Washington, D.C.
That is the capital of the United States.

The President lives in a big house
called the White House.

Several United States Presidents
are from North Carolina!

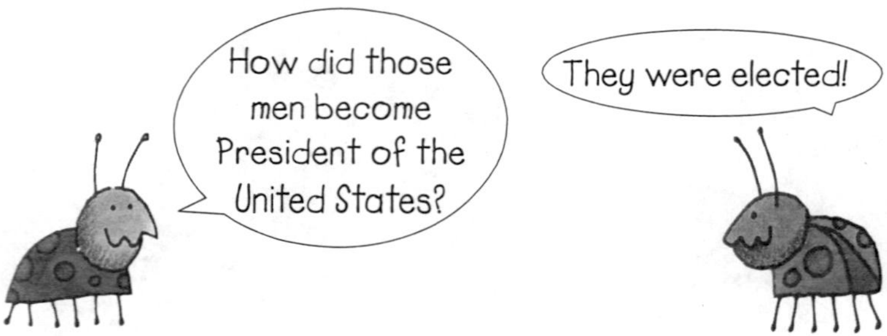

Andrew Jackson
7th President
James K. Polk
11th President
Andrew Johnson
17th President

PEOPLE

Many famous people

Virginia Dare

First English baby born in the New World

Dolley Madison

First Lady and wife of President James Madison

William Sydney Porter

Short story writer known as "O. Henry"

call our state home!

Let's hang out!

PEOPLE

Billy Graham
World-famous minister

Maya Angelou
Writer and poet

Michael Jordan
Olympic gold medalist and NBA star

Cardinal

BIRD

I am the state bird, and I fly
over North Carolina, proud and high.

As I fly, up in the sky,
I flap my wings to tell you "Hi!"

The North Carolina state bird is the Cardinal.

Dogwood

I am the Dogwood.
I am the state flower.

I grow where it's warm and sunny.
I bloom in early spring.
I help make North Carolina beautiful!

Look at me! Smell me!
My blooms are white and
red and pink!

FLOWER

Pine

TREE

I am a Pine—I'm the state tree.
All over North Carolina you can find me.

My roots run deep, they keep me strong.
My leaves stay green, all year long.

I stand up straight, big and tall.
Don't climb too high—it would hurt to fall!

Honeybee

INSECT

I am the Honeybee.
I am the state insect.

I might sting you if you bother me,
But really, I am your friend.

I carry pollen from flower to flower.
I make honey.
I help North Carolina crops grow.

BZZZZZZZZZZZZ!

Atlantic Ocean

Let's go to the beach!

We can swim in the waves.
We can play in the sand.

We can build a big castle
where water meets land.

North Carolina's barrier islands
are home to many animals:

Sea Turtles **Sharks** **Birds** **Crabs** **Dolphins** **and More!**

BEACHES

Appalachian Mountains

MOUNTAINS

North Carolina's Appalachian Mountains
are the place to be.
Hiking, fishing, camping—
fun for you and me.

If you were to climb
to the top of a tree,
you might be able to see Tennessee!

Nantahala National Forest

FORESTS

North Carolina has many beautiful forests. The Nantahala National Forest is the largest one. It is in southwest North Carolina.

This habitat is home to many animals:

Birds Deer Snakes Black Bears Owls and More!

The Nantahala National Forest has trees that are hundreds of years old!

Biltmore Estate
I call that room on the fourth floor!
I wanted that one!

The Biltmore Estate is the largest house in the United States!
It is in Asheville.

George W. Vanderbilt built the house in 1895.
It has 250 rooms!

There are 65 fireplaces and three kitchens in the Biltmore Estate!

LANDMARK

North Carolina Crops

AGRICULTURE

North Carolina has many farms.
Why?
Because North Carolina has good soil
and a warm climate!

Some of the crops grown in North Carolina are:

Tobacco | **Sweet Potatoes**
Cotton | **Soybeans**

Hey!
Don't forget about me!
I am a North Carolina Christmas tree.

My state is #2 in growing Christmas trees.
Ho Ho Ho! Merry Christmas!

Sports in North Carolina

SPORTS

Baseball! Basketball! Football!
North Carolina has it all.

Whether you like to watch or play,
You are sure to have a ball!

Panthers

Hornets

Hurricanes

Tar Heels

Blue Devils

& More!

North Carolina: First in Flight

The first airplane flight took place at Kitty Hawk, North Carolina.

Kitty Hawk was chosen because it is always windy there. The first flight lasted 12 seconds!

Wilbur and Orville Wright invented the airplane!

CLAIM TO FAME

GLOSSARY

climate: weather conditions in an area over a long period of time

elect: to choose someone by voting

estate: a very big house on a large piece of land

habitat: a place where plants or animals naturally live

invent: to create something that has not existed before

laws: rules made by the government

pollen: a yellow powder that helps plants make new plants

region: an area that has similar characteristics

settlement: the first community in an area

tar: a dark, thick, sticky liquid used to make roads